Markings on the Windowsill

"I have known Ron for thirty-five years, and he is made of the 'real stuff.' He enables the reader to deal with 'real stuff' through his book. Readers will be amazed at the hope this book produces on each page."

—*Don Harp,*
senior minister, Peachtree Road United Methodist Church

"*Markings on the Windowsill* is sacred ground. . . . Be *careful* with this book . . . when you pick it up, go to a very quiet place, and plan to be there a while. God will speak to you. Your life will be changed. I promise."

—*Bill Curry,*
ESPN sports analyst and speaker

MARKINGS
on the Windowsill

A Book About Grief That's Really About Hope

RONALD J. GREER

Abingdon Press

MARKINGS ON THE WINDOWSILL
A BOOK ABOUT GRIEF THAT'S REALLY ABOUT HOPE

Copyright © 2006 by Dimensions for Living

All rights reserved.

This book is printed on acid-free paper.

Library of Congress Cataloging-in-Publication Data

Greer, Ronald J., 1947-
    Markings on the windowsill : a book about grief that's really about hope / Ronald J. Greer.
        p. cm.
    ISBN 0-687-33363-6 (binding: adhesive, perfect : alk. paper)
    1. Consolation. 2. Grief—Religious aspects—Christianity. 3. Bereavement—Religious aspects—Christianity. 4. Greer, Ronald J., 1947-
    I. Title.
    BV4905.3.G735 2006
    248.8'66—dc22

                                                                2006012595

All scripture quotations unless noted otherwise are taken from the *New Revised Standard Version of the Bible,* copyright 1989, by the Division of Christian Education of the National Council of the Churches of Christ in the United States of America. Used by permission. All rights reserved.

Scripture marked KJV is from the King James or Authorized Version of the Bible.

Scripture marked RSV is from the *Revised Standard Version of the Bible,* copyright 1946, 1952, 1971 by the Division of Christian Education of the National Council of the Churches of Christ in the United States of America. Used by permission. All rights reserved.

Scripture marked ASV is from the American Standard Version of the Bible.

06 07 08 09 10 11 12 13 14 15—10 9 8 7 6 5 4 3 2 1

MANUFACTURED IN THE UNITED STATES OF AMERICA

To Karen,
from whom I have learned of
courage, hope, and grace
in the midst of unspeakable grief.

And to our children,
Patrick, Eric, and Brooke,
who have filled our home with
joy and love.

Contents

Prologue

I am writing for you who grieve.

A beautiful fall afternoon suddenly turned tragic . . . and changed our lives forever. A truck hit our car and left my family scattered across a highway. Our two-year-old son died. His name is Eric.

As a father, a Christian, and a minister, I am aware that many writings on grief encourage denial of our sadness since our loved ones have "gone to a better place." That is true and an enormous relief. But what about those of us left in this place? I am writing to you who have been left and are longing for ways to give a voice to your pain. I am writing on how we can grieve and in the process become transformed.

This is a book on grief, but it's really about hope.

Moments by the Window

. . . *with hands outstretched toward the window.*
—*Tobit 3:11*

E*ric was not yet two and was all boy. He loved adven-
ture. He liked to try things out. And he had a pen. We had
just moved into our new home. The freshly painted woodwork around the dining room windows looked like a great
canvas to this budding artist. He let his creative juices
flow.*

*I stood there that evening looking at the marks all over
the woodwork and the windowsill. They were drawn with
authority, etched deeply into the wood. They couldn't be
washed off. I was less than pleased.*

*Four months later I was standing in front of that same
window, looking at those same markings. This time there
was no anger. This time there were only tears.*

*Eric had died tragically in the accident. Our older son,
Patrick, was in the hospital with his leg in traction. My
wife, Karen, and I were practically living there with him. I
had gone home one evening soon after Eric's funeral to get
clothes and check on the house.*

It was quiet. It felt empty. All I could think of was Eric. I walked through the house crying, remembering. I paused for several minutes in the small yellow bedroom that had been his. I sat on his bed. I picked up his pillow to smell it one more time.

It was time to go. I turned out the lights as I went past each room. I stepped into the dining room to reach for the switch. And there it was: the window. There before me was Eric's art. Those same markings had gone from being a blemish to being priceless.

I couldn't leave without touching it. I knelt there rubbing the woodwork, following the lines our son had drawn. I treasured every curve and slant he'd marked into that painted wood.

I could picture the pen in his little hand, the wrinkle of his brow as he bent to do his drawing. It would never be painted over. It would be forever Eric's signature.

His markings connected me with him. I hated to leave them. I wasn't ready to go. But then, I hadn't been ready for any of this.

Psychologist Carl Rogers wrote in *On Becoming a Person,* "I have almost invariably found that the very feeling which has seemed to me most private, most personal . . . has turned out to be an expression for which there is a resonance in many other people. . . . What is most personal and unique in each one of us is probably the very element which would . . . speak most deeply to others" (Boston: Houghton Mifflin, 1961, p. 26).

It is in that spirit that I offer what I have learned—in the hope that it might resonate with you and your experience. I offer these writings both as a person who has known profound loss and as a pastoral counselor who has been with countless others in their losses.

I am indebted to those who have allowed me the privilege of listening to their life stories. From them I have learned much of what it means to live courageously with grief.

My intention here is to write this as a conversation with a friend. I write much of this in the second person. I am writing to you. These reflections need not be read first to last. Read the ones that speak to you.

I have waited years to put my thoughts into writing. I did not want to bleed on every page. Instead, I wanted these words to be useful to you, so I waited until I had healed more fully and could reflect on all that I had experienced. I did not want to report as a journalist from the intensity of the battle scene; the emotion would be profound, but the perspective limited.

Perhaps now I am ready. Perhaps.

It has been over two decades now since Eric's death. I am still learning to live with my loss.

Also involved in the accident were Karen, Patrick, and our sitter, whom Karen had picked up just moments before. All were injured. Patrick, who had his femur badly broken, would be months in healing.

The emotional healing has taken years for all of us. In fact, it continues still. There is wisdom in the old saying, "There are some losses you never get over. You simply discover how best you will live with them."

This is my experience. Perhaps it resonates with your own.

The Valley

Yea, though I walk through the valley of the shadow
of death, I will fear no evil: for thou art with me.
—Psalm 23:4 KJV

K aren was to meet me at an intersection outside of Atlanta, where we would leave together for a speaking engagement in the North Georgia mountains. She was to pick up a sitter for our sons, let them off at home, and then meet me. I waited. The appointed time had passed. There were no cell phones with which to call.

I waited. What had begun as irritation gave way to concern. I knew something was wrong. From a service-station pay phone I called my administrative assistant at the church. I remember her words to me clearly: "Thank God you called. There has been a terrible accident—"

My grief began.

The word *grief* sounds too small for all we are feeling. That one simple word is asked to carry so much emotion—so much sadness, emptiness, loneliness, confusion, heartbreak, pain. All of this, and so much more, is what we mean by *grief*.

It is understandable that the word *grief* comes from the Latin *gravis*, which means "heavy." Any time I am experiencing my grief I am aware of the accuracy of its word origin. I feel the weight of the loss. My energy is sapped by the burden.

Grief involves mourning and anguish. It involves the loss of someone or perhaps something that had a special place in your heart. Grief involves death, either literal or metaphorical. It means saying "good-bye." It brings tears. It takes time.

The term *grief* actually refers to the experience of loss, while the term *mourning* refers to how those feelings of loss are expressed. Grief is the blow that hits you; mourning is how you respond, how you work through those emotions and give them traction. It is common to use the two terms interchangeably, and I do the same. Still, it is useful to know that there is a difference between the experience and the expression. We have no choice about suffering the loss, but we have freedom in deciding how we will handle the suffering. We have to experience the grief. But *mourning* is a choice—and a very wise one.

To speak of "the grief process" is so very clichéd, but grief is indeed a process, a journey through which we must go. In a society that abhors anything that cannot be done quickly, this process, to be done successfully, takes time—often months, sometimes years.

My focus throughout this book is largely on the emotions that result from the death of a loved one. Yet, grief is hardly limited to physical death. Any significant loss—of a dream, a relationship, an ability—is a kind of death, and grief is experienced. Much in this book will apply to those suffering grief or loss of any kind.

We feel pain with any important loss. We mourn. The more profound the importance of who or what was lost, the more profound the grief. To express such grief is absolutely crucial. There are no shortcuts. Suppressing our emotions, pushing them down and out of the way because "I'm supposed to be past this by now" or rationalizing that "her death was really a blessing for her anyway" is ultimately a futile effort.

As time passes we find we are living atop a reservoir of old pain long collected. More and more effort is needed to keep it packed down as the pressure builds. We are left tired, lethargic, unfocused, and disinterested in what had before been meaningful. We become less available to those around us. In other words, we are experiencing the classic signs of depression.

If you want to see grief handled this way, watch the movie *Ordinary People* and study the character of Beth Jarrett, played so well by Mary Tyler Moore. Following the drowning death of her son, Beth quickly moved on with her life in order to avoid the pain. Look into her face—her hardened, rigid face. You see both her depression and her anger. Listen to her voice—not the lyrics, but the score. She speaks with the staccato rhythm of suppressed grief and unexpressed rage.

Suppression can bring depression, but expression can bring a kind of resurrection. A friend once said, "Most of us aren't willing to hang on our crosses long enough to experience resurrection." Most of us want to hurry by the terrible pain. We don't want to feel the pain of the loss. Yet that very experience is what enables us to get to the other side.

Give your grief a voice. Cry it out. Talk it out. Write it out if you find journaling to be valuable. Express it as it comes. Keep it current. Giving a voice to your pain enables the wound to heal.

Again, scripture shares its wisdom: "Weeping may linger for the night, / but joy comes with the morning" (Psalm 30:5). It is a joy that is earned—one that comes out of having the courage to feel what you feel, and to mourn the depth of the loss that is before you.

Your grief cannot be hurried. Take your time. Joy will come, with the morning.

The Rock at the Bottom

Blessed are those who mourn, for they shall be comforted. —Matthew 5:4 RSV

I remember too well the pain. The awful, gut-wrenching pain. The sobs. The kind of crying that goes on and on and on. The heartache. Literal. Real. Not a metaphor. My chest aching from the sheer physical effort of it all.

I remember. The hours spent at the cemetery over Eric's grave. Sobbing. Talking to him of how much I loved him, of how much I missed him. Of how empty I felt without him. The tears came and would not stop.

I remember. The cemetery in the pitch-black dark of night as I came to let out more pain. I cried best alone, when I didn't have to take care of anyone, anyone but myself. I must have looked crazy out there in the middle of the night. I was. Crazy in my grief. The hurt was so deep. It was like something toxic that I had to get out of my system, or something inside me would die.

Grieving is an act of enormous courage.

To grieve well requires a willingness to open yourself to the depth of your pain. It can be a frightening experience. There are many who simply do not choose to go there. I have heard some speak of their anxiety about "letting go" and giving in to their grief out of a fear of being swept away in it. It seems like a bottomless pit into which they could fall forever.

That has not been my experience. I remember a comment made when several persons were consoling a friend who had been through a very difficult time. She said she simply had hit rock bottom. There was a pause, and one person in the group said, "But isn't it good to know when you hit rock bottom, that at the bottom there is a rock?"

My experience is that there *is* a rock at the bottom. At the depth of our grief and pain, we arrive at a place within us that feels grounded. Ironically, the way to find that substantial footing is to be willing to "sink" into experiencing the pain—to be willing to have the courage to take on your grief as it comes and to hold nothing back.

To mourn fully and to mourn well is to allow yourself to be genuine. It is to be all that you are and to feel all that you feel. This is working through your pain, not wallowing in it. As you work through your grief, you will live out of a greater spiritual and emotional depth than you have ever experienced. You are at a level within yourself that is of greater substance, strength, and maturity than you have ever known. You are in the presence of God. It is surely this spiritual place to which the psalmist was referring: "He only is my rock and my salvation, / my fortress; I shall not be greatly moved" (Psalm 62:2 RSV).

Some grief researchers have found that persons of faith tend to grieve their losses with more passion just after the death than persons who are not spiritual. Follow-up studies show that two years later, the spiritual persons, having expressed their grief more intensely, are doing better than the nonspiritual persons. They tend to work through their grief more readily and perhaps more successfully.

I believe this is connected with the insight of the Apostle Paul, who wrote, "We do not want you to be uninformed, brothers and sisters, about those who have died, so that you may not grieve as others do who have no hope" (1 Thessalonians 4:13). As Christians, we grieve as those with hope. We grieve with the faith and the hope that we are supported by the grace of a deeply loving God—the God who is the rock at the bottom. We sink into the sadness and the despair knowing the grounding is there; that no matter how dark the valley, God is with us.

I distinguish this kind of active mourning from passive hurting. Many times people have come to see me for counseling regarding their depression. On some of these occasions I feel that their depression may be related to a major loss that has occurred sometime earlier in their lives. I ask about the deaths they have known and how fully they have grieved these losses. Sometimes I hear, "Oh, I hurt with it for years."

I do not minimize the depth of their pain, but often what we discover is that they were not getting it out. They weren't giving a voice to their grief. Active mourning means expressing the pain. It means to let out your tears, and to talk to dear and trusted friends. Passive hurting is more like an internal retreat—a withdrawal into your self. Its focus is more of an effort to cope, rather than working through the grief.

As Christians, we also grieve as those with another hope. We grieve as those with the faith in a spiritual realm into which the soul of the one we loved has now entered. No matter how deep our pain, as persons of faith we can grieve without the concern of their well-being to distract or burden us. We can pour out the pain for our own loss knowing that our loved one is well and in the loving care of God.

As Paul wrote, "You may not grieve as others do who have no hope." His words are both an affirmation of faith and an affirmation of the need to work through the pain.

The Journey

*I am weary with my moaning; / every night I flood
my bed with tears. —Psalm 6:6*

I didn't want time to budge. With each passing day I
would be a day farther away from the time when I had held
him and played with him. Would my memory of the details
fade? I wondered. Would I forget the sound of his voice or
the smell of the back of his neck?

I didn't want time to budge. It was late October when
Eric died. The leaves were changing. I looked out the back
window one afternoon a few days later and saw that many
of the leaves had fallen. The world was changing. Life was
going on without him. I was that much farther away from
him. It was a crazy moment. I desperately wanted to put
the leaves back on those bare limbs.

But the journey had begun and would not stop just
because I wished it so.

Nearly every book on grief has the obligatory "stages"
chapter that walks through the process of grief, alerting
the reader to the emotions one likely is to expect. At the

risk of fitting the formula, I include this brief chapter for any who may fear you are crazy in your grieving. Of course you are. It's a part of the process. But you are not alone.

Psychiatrist Elisabeth Kübler-Ross, in her book *On Death and Dying*, wrote of the stages of grief as applied to a terminally ill person. "Stages" may have been an unfortunate choice of words; there are no neat, predictable stages. Your experience depends on much that is distinctive to the uniqueness of your life. What was your relationship with the person who died? How close, how meaningful was the relationship? How long was the relationship? How did your loved one die? Was it expected or was it sudden, with all of the grief coming after the unanticipated death?

Though the grief journey is unique for each of us, there are broad parallels that most find in common. There are phases of emotion you can expect. They are not precise. They overlap. But grief is a process, and there is a *moving ahead*—though it is painfully slow.

These phases are not neat and orderly. You can expect to drift back from your current phase into emotions associated with an earlier one. In my grief I have never known to which emotion I might awaken next.

I once read a sports column about the unique personality of a college basketball coach. This coach was a brilliant man who would sprinkle wide-ranging quotes throughout his interviews. The columnist wrote that listening to him talk was like listening to an AM radio on scan.

Similarly, I find that my heart may land on any emotion at any given time. My grief is always on scan. Many find this process to be a cycle they revisit over and over again. Yet, it isn't regression. There is movement. There is healing. Grief that has gone awry, "complicated grief" as it is called, is seen when someone becomes emotionally arrested for an extended period in one of these phases. Professional help may be needed when, over time, there isn't a sense of process toward healing.

I want to present briefly these phases you may expect. Again, every grief experience is unique. These are markers, guideposts you will not be surprised to feel on the journey.

Each of these phases is an area of emotion those who grieve tend to move into, work through, work out of, and occasionally revisit.

Shock and Numbness

"It can't be. It can't be true. It just can't be true" is heard as the voice trails off, the eyes dazed and downcast.

This woman is in shock trying to process the heartbreaking news she has just heard. She is shaking her head or staring into space, struggling to come to terms with what she has just learned.

The blow is obviously more pronounced when the death is sudden and unexpected. You go from a world in which the person you love is prominent to a world where he or she is so tragically absent.

Yet, this feeling of devastation can occur even in cases where the death has been expected for months. As many have been heard to say, "You think you're ready for it, and then—" There is something about the reality hitting you that may take you by surprise.

Initially, there may be disbelief and even denial: "You are wrong. You didn't get the message straight. How dare you tell me he was killed." As an initial reaction, this is not at all unhealthy. This person's pain is so great and his or her world is about to be so radically changed, that this pause is needed before the news can be accepted and acknowledged.

The denial may transition into a time of yearning and pleading: "Please, God, don't let this be true." Unconsciously, the process has been engaged. The grieving person is out of denial but is not ready to take on the full brunt of the impact of the loss. He or she is biting off only as much as can be chewed at one time.

Flood of Grief

In this phase, the loss is felt with full force. The pain hits so hard. Any shock has worn off, and there is no anesthesia. This is a time of intense suffering. Endless tears. Wave after wave of incredible pain. Nights filled with much sobbing and little sleep. Feelings of deep emptiness and loneliness.

The pain won't go away. Many have described to me the feeling of "going through the motions." Even on the good days it's simply putting one foot in front of the other. For others there is a sense of disorientation.

Anger is often felt during this time. It may be exaggerated, and its focus may seem random. It is the rage of protest coming out of the pain of the loss and fear of the future. It may be aimed at the person who died ("How could you leave me?") or at God ("How could you take him so soon?") or at a target more randomly selected ("With decent medical care he'd still be alive").

Or the grieving person may focus the anger inward and experience terrible guilt. It is usually about words said and unsaid, or things done or left undone. It is often an exaggerated and unrealistic guilt, significantly out of proportion to what one would feel under normal circumstances.

Despair

This is the phase of the long haul. The initial grieving has been done, and the grieving person settles in for the dull sadness. In the case of a spouse who has died, this is when the survivor faces each of the significant events the two had enjoyed together—only now alone.

Though the surviving spouse may not often be overwhelmed anymore in this phase, there is so little pleasure in life. For example, the widow may not be quite as obsessed with her loss as earlier, but it is never far from her mind. Her life feels empty. She is not in denial, but life often feels unreal—like some awful dream from which she surely will awaken. As she goes through her day the loss is always in the back of her mind. A random reminder will quickly bring it to center stage. When she awakens in the morning, it is still the first thought she has.

Often she has times of restlessness during which she can't quite put a finger on what is wrong. What is wrong is that life still feels awkward and off-balance. Frequently, fatigue is experienced as she is reminded of just how much work is involved in this process.

Then one day, totally unexpectedly, she laughs. In the company of a good friend something amusing is said, and she laughs out loud. To the rest of the world this might seem inconsequential, but it's the first time she has laughed in so long. There may be a twinge of guilt. *How can I be enjoying myself with my husband dead?* she likely will ask herself. Hopefully, she then will realize that she has begun to move ahead and will give herself permission to do so.

Integration and Affirmation

This phase is long in coming. It begins after the loss has been fully and painfully experienced, the mourning has been engaged, and many tears have been shed. The grieving person is arriving in a new place. She is integrating the life she knew with the one she now lives. She continues to redefine the content and shape of that life— her "new normal" as it is often called. She carries the love she knew with her husband into her new world. She is integrating, assimilating both her loss and the memories of the life they shared. Her husband is achieving his place in her heart and memory as she courageously moves forward with her life.

This is a different life, but one to be affirmed. She feels meaning and fulfillment again. She has accepted her life without the one she loved. The pain still surfaces, and the tears still come. For important losses, there is no final closure. She has discovered that mourning is not a task to be completed but a process to be engaged. Yet, she wakes up on most mornings and feels good. His death isn't always her first thought. She has begun to move forward with courage and resiliency. There is new purpose, hope, and direction. She is enjoying life again. She is discovering her life to be transformed.

As I write this, my wife, Karen, has just returned from a visit with her parents. She brought back some photographs they found of Eric's second birthday party. We loved seeing them. We remembered that day. We remembered the fun we had that afternoon sitting on the floor watching him unwrap his gifts. We could hear his delighted voice again as he opened each present. There he was with our English Cocker. Her name was Apple—"Babble" was as close as he could pronounce it. We remembered our Eric. The tender awareness of all we had lost was clearly in the background as we celebrated his young and brief life.

When the healing has been substantially attained, we intuitively think first of the *life* of our loved ones, and then of their deaths.

Respect the Seasons That Will Come

For everything there is a season, and a time for
every matter under heaven:
a time to be born, and a time to die; . . .
a time to weep, and a time to laugh;
a time to mourn, and a time to dance.
—Ecclesiastes 3:1-2, 4

I never knew how powerfully the seasons would come. Eric died on October 20th. A month later I was standing in the shower and for no known reason began to cry. I had not been thinking of Eric or the ordeal we were going through. But I began to cry. Then it dawned on me. I felt the pain at just the moment when, one month before, we had been told Eric was clinically dead.

A month after that, on December 20th, I was talking with someone just before noon. Suddenly, in mid-sentence, my mind went completely blank. Slowly in the silence it dawned on me that this was, again, the 20th—the date of Eric's death. I apologized to the person with whom I had been speaking and had to be reminded of what we were saying. Several minutes later, walking to lunch, I realized *that my mind had gone blank at precisely the moment when, two months before, we had been told from the EEG that Eric's mind was blank.*

There are always seasons to our lives. There is a rhythm, a tempo. There is an ebb and flow to emotions.

So it is with grief. It tends to come in like the tide of an ocean. Each wave contains memories and pain and emptiness and loss. There is almost a rhythm to it. A season will come, and then it will go to make room for another. Some we sense coming; others take us by surprise.

We know to expect the anniversaries to be especially emotional times. It may be the anniversary of a loved one's death or birth, or it may be a wedding anniversary. We can expect the tide to come in on those annual seasons. It is often a powerful experience. For many, the date of the month—every month for the first year or so— can bring back the intensity of the loss.

Having grieved so fully for a year or two, or more, you may be surprised on that special day that the feeling of loss hits so hard. "But I thought I was over it." No, not over it, just working through it. It is a process, one with seasons. They can't be hurried any more than we could rush a sunrise.

The waves of emotion will also come on those occasions when families gather for a special celebration. In how many weddings have I officiated where there was a specific mention in the bulletin that the roses on the altar were in memory of the grandparents whose names were listed?

If a father has died prior to his daughter's wedding, the bride likely will need to honor her grief at his important absence on her special day. Someone else will be walking her down the aisle. Graduations, weddings, baptisms are all occasions where one may feel a special tenderness for loved ones who will not be there.

When parents lose a child they will always be aware of what his or her age would have been at any given point in time. They will know which particular birthday it is in any given year. Often they will be especially aware of their child's classmates, knowing when they move on to high school, when they graduate, when they finish college, and when they marry. Along with the celebration and happiness for the friends they had known, there is a secret, unspoken sadness for what will never be.

The Empty Chair

Another of the expected waves comes with the holidays. There is so much wisdom to the notion of the "year of mourning." Within that year, each of the special days for the family is experienced for the first time without their loved one there. It is the experience of "the empty chair"—no matter how many chairs are filled, it is the empty one that is the focus.

The holidays are a wonderful time to work through the grief together. Instead of ignoring what everyone around the table is thinking, give it a voice: "You know, I was just remembering the time that Grandma . . ." and suddenly the family is alive with emotion. Stories are told and events are remembered about someone so dear. Laughter is heard. A tear quietly sneaks down someone's cheek. Out of it all—the telling and the remembering—family members have helped each other work through a bit more of their grief and honored Grandma's memory in a most personal way.

The First Christmas

It will be difficult for those experiencing their first Christmas without someone they dearly loved. Let me offer some brief suggestions.

- *Cry early.* Know that you need to grieve going into the holidays; the pain will not subside without it. This may make you as emotionally available as possible to truly enjoy the parts of the season you can. Don't wait for Christmas to arrive and then let the grief hit you. Be open to how you feel as the holidays approach. Holiday grief that is successfully denied will usually leave you in an even deeper postholiday depression.
- *Have realistic expectations.* This Christmas will not be the same. It will be lonely. Lower your expectations for this one. Even if you don't feel it is going

to be much of a holiday, make the most you can of it.

- *Plan ahead.* Plan to surround yourself with those who are good for you and enrich you. Do as few obligatory engagements as possible. Schedule your holidays in ways that will work for you. You may have the same plans as before, or they may be different. The question should be, Does this work best for me? In a manner of speaking, this needs to be *your* Christmas. Design it your way, without a hint of guilt.

You may decide to do your holiday differently. Life has changed for you and your family. You are in a new and different place. The question is not Who are we? but Who are we now—in this new context? Who are we as a family now? How have we changed? What will we do differently?

The year after our loss, we decided that we weren't going to just sit around the house as, now, a family of three and think about Eric. We had been grieving plenty, so this wasn't motivated by denial. We figured our choices were to be at home and be sad, or to travel and enjoy the time together as best we could. We decided to take off. Thanksgiving that following year was spent at Disney World, and many succeeding holidays were spent doing whatever we felt we would enjoy. We found new and meaningful ways of being together on those special occasions.

Each of the waves of emotion we feel—whether related to an anniversary or a holiday or any special day—needs to be "tended" and taken seriously. Each comes out of the deep inner wisdom within ourselves that says, *It's time now to get back to "work," to grieve some more.* I think of it as keeping our grief "current." If we ignore that message, the grief backs up, and depression is often the result.

But if we pay attention to that inner wisdom and grieve when each of these waves of pain comes in—and in that way keep our grief current—we then tend to find the waves beginning to change in three different ways with the passing of time. They tend to come in less frequently, they hit less powerfully, and they begin to recede more quickly.

When you have a powerful loss in your life, expect the seasons to come. As they do, grieve them, and grieve them well.

Tragedy Makes No Sense

No one has power over the wind to restrain the wind, or power over the day of death.
—Ecclesiastes 8:8

A pastor friend was standing with me as a woman introduced herself the week after Eric died. She was obviously feeling the need to say something supportive but struggling with what to say. Finally, she spoke of Eric's death being God's will, though we may not understand it. She then wished me well and excused herself.

My friend leaned over to me and whispered, "Greer, if God killed your boy, I'm hanging up my robe."

Some hold the view that meaning is to be found in tragedy. If God is in charge, there must be a purpose to whatever event has taken place. All kinds of motives are projected onto God in heartbreaking circumstances. We have heard them countless times in funeral homes: "It was all a part of God's will"; "God wanted her all for himself"; "God picks the loveliest of flowers"; "God took him for a purpose"; or "We are not to ask 'why'; God knows what he is doing."

Many believe this. Others are simply anxious and wanting to find a positive spin that may help a grieving friend feel better.

Those who believe in this theology look to the results of tragedy. They point to all the growth that comes out of genuinely heartbreaking situations and easily see God as the cause behind it all. We all have known of those times when such an experience has been used as a wake-up call to a life thereafter lived with a new focus and meaning.

I recall reading years ago the story of a couple who had a developmentally disabled child who died very young. To them, this was God's doing: God had made their child disabled and caused her death to get their attention and to bring them into more spiritual lives.

We can understand, of course, how it would seem that way. To see lives turned around, to see all the good that can come out of tragedy—surely God must have caused the death for the sake of those who continued to live.

I don't think so.

I see no inherent meaning in tragedy, though I see much meaning that can come out of it. God doesn't cause heartache to teach lessons. That is not his style for helping us grow. God doesn't cause heartache, and he is not a murderer. God loves us. He doesn't beat us up to help us learn.

"But," the protest may well be lodged, "how can you explain all the positive—the good, the spiritual, the growth—that results?"

I return to an old adage (one that violates my long-held philosophy that there is little wisdom in anything that rhymes). It has been said, "God can use what he didn't choose." The Christian faith consistently points to a God who would not cause pain for anyone, but who is there to bring growth and new life out of the pain that does come. It is very much God's style to bring resurrections out of life's crucifixions.

Better Questions Than *"Why?"*

I have no problem with those who ponder the question *"Why?"* in the event of tragedy. It is a question that simply does not seem answerable—perhaps because there *is* no "why." More useful questions may be *"How?"* and *"What?"*

How am I going to grow from this powerful experience in my life? How can I allow God to use this moment so that I can become a more authentic, substantial, and caring person? Having visited the very depth of my soul, what can I bring back to enrich and deepen the living of my life? What can I learn? What can I take with me?

In his book *Creative Suffering*, Dr. Paul Tournier put it this way: "Good and evil, in the moral sense, do not reside in things, but always in persons. Things and events, whether fortunate or unfortunate, are simply what they are, morally neutral. What matters is the way we react to them. Only rarely are we the masters of events, but (along with those who help us) we are responsible for our reactions" (San Francisco: Harper & Row, 1981, p. 29).

I have looked for meaning in Eric's dying. There is none. It was a tragic collision of vehicles. There is no inherent meaning in it. But there can be meaning in how I respond to it. Out of his death there can be—and has been—new life in me. Out of his death I became more than I ever had been.

Where Is God in This?

For he makes his sun rise on the evil and on the good, and sends rain on the righteous and on the unrighteous. —Matthew 5:45

I never felt alone. Throughout the entire nightmare, I never felt I was by myself. I was in the greatest pain I had ever known, not knowing what our lives would look like when the dust finally settled—but always I felt a certainty. I felt anchored. Anchored in the conviction that I was grounded by something greater than myself, something supportive and profoundly gracious.

What I struggle to describe is so subtle. Yet, it is important beyond words. In my deepest, darkest moments there was— even if over in a far corner—always a light. A presence. A spiritual presence. A light shining in the darkness.

It is written that God speaks in a still, small voice. To me his presence never dominated. In the chaos of that time, it was rarely the focus of my attention. Yet, it always was there, in the background, softly spoken. Reminding me that Eric was all right. And that one day, we would be too.

"My faith has really been shaken by this," is often heard following a tragedy. Implied in this is a correlation between our goodness and how God would allow life to treat us. But Jesus never said if we were good, then life would be good. We know it just doesn't work that way.

I have no idea why much of the world is created the way it is. I feel much the same way as a friend of mine who says, "When I cross the Jordan, I'm going with questions." There is a randomness to life. Accidents happen. Tragedies occur. Young lives are cut short. It makes no sense. When my friend and I do cross the Jordan, we likely will have to get in line with our questions.

What we do know is that there are certain principles that are in place. Diseases strike. Floods rage. Cars violently crash into each other. Tragedy may result from the invasion of these realities into our world. But it is not the will of God. It is simply the by-product of basic principles of this world crashing painfully into our lives. Life plays no favorites. In Matthew, Jesus said, "For [God] makes his sun rise on the evil and on the good, and sends rain on the righteous and on the unrighteous" (5:45).

For those whose faith has been shaken, I believe what actually has been shaken is their understanding of who God is and how God relates with us. In their pain, they are on the threshold of moving into a deeper and more mature faith.

No one who prays through the night for his dying child to live, then watches the sunrise still in prayer, goes through life without an altered view of God.

He is not the grand puppeteer who pulls strings so that his favorites get their way. The rain falls and the sun shines on us all. He doesn't alter events to make them all right. Rather, he gives us the grace and strength to make it through what we did not know we could survive.

In addition to the randomness in life, there also is free will. We were created to be in relationship with God. To be in a relationship requires freedom. In order to say "yes" there must be the opportunity of saying "no." Free will is the option to choose—wisely or not. If a decision is poorly made, if tragedy happens, it may be a mistake made from the freedom God gave us—but it was not his call. It was not his will.

The idea of tragedy being God's will is a contradiction to every word Jesus spoke of God. "Do you want to see God?" Jesus might well have asked. "Then let me tell you a story: 'There was a man who had two sons—'" And on goes the parable of the father and his sons, the elder and the prodigal (Luke 15:11-32).

The father in the parable certainly allowed his younger son free will, but he was also longing, waiting expectantly for that moment when, as the scriptures say, the son "came to himself" (v. 17), when he returned to the integrity of who he was. He is the parent who stands waiting and watching for his son to come home. That is the spirit and attitude of God. He allows us the freedom to live as we choose—but passionately wants the very best for us.

Then where is God in our grief? In the life of Jesus, we get the single clearest glimpse of the nature of God as he was moved to tears at others' pain. *Where is God in this?* Grieving with us. Supporting us, loving us. And having also had a son tragically killed, he identifies with us every step of the way.

The Need to Grieve in One's Own Way

But as for me, I walk in my integrity.
—Psalm 26:11

The second EEG was flat, just as we had expected. We had made our decision to take our son off the ventilator if, in fact, he already was dead. I had one request of our physician. When it was turned off I wanted to be holding our son. This was the only way to do it that had integrity for me. He would go from one loving father to another. It was arranged.

There is no description for walking into your son's hospital room for the final time. Two chairs had been placed beside his bed for us. All but one of the tubes had been taken out. Karen and I sat together. A kind and quiet nurse lifted Eric from his bed and gently laid him in Karen's arms. She held him, kissed him, and—after a time—gave him to me.

I thought it would happen much faster. With no oxygen being forced into his little body I assumed his heart would quickly stop. For almost half an hour we cried and talked with our son of our love for him. We said "good-bye" with him in my arms. It was the only way we could do it.

"I wish I had done it all differently," so many people have said to me through the years. The moment of good-bye comes so quickly, yet lingers for so long. Surely some profound words or actions are needed. But there is no script, no prescribed ritual.

Many people with whom I have talked over the years have expressed regrets. They wish they had done something differently. Something that would have had a unique meaning for them. Some deed, some word spoken, some symbolic act that would have been a step, a move toward saying good-bye.

Instead, they did what was expected, what was appropriate. But it did not fit them. It did not have integrity for them. The word *integrity* means to be whole, where you live in harmony with yourself—where your thinking, your feeling, your living are in sync. Many find that following what is "socially acceptable" for grieving just does not fit; it has no integrity for them. When they follow the norm instead of their hearts, they go through life with a secret regret.

Eric's first EEG had been done. It was flat. There was no brain activity. He likely had died instantly, and only the ventilator was keeping his heart beating. A second EEG would be done, but there was little doubt as to the outcome. Our son Patrick, who was six, was down the hall in traction from the accident. His femur had been broken completely.

We wanted to offer Patrick the opportunity to say "good-bye" to his little brother. They had a wonderful relationship. They played together. They got on each other's nerves. They laughed together. At times the kid brother was a joy, at other times a real pest. They were a couple of typical brothers who loved each other dearly. So it was important that one brother be given the chance to say his good-bye to the other. It also would be valuable for Patrick to see that, although Eric was no longer the towheaded little guy running across the yard, he also no longer looked as he did when Patrick last saw him on that highway.

It was Patrick's choice. He accepted. The emotion of the moment was powerful as the bed of this young boy was wheeled to the doorway of his brother's room. Patrick said his "good-bye."

We had to do it our way. We had to offer him the opportunity. We had to grieve in ways that felt right to us.

You must grieve in ways that are right for you. Open the casket or leave it closed. Have a funeral or a memorial service or a simple graveside service. Visit the cemetery every day or once a month. It doesn't matter. It doesn't matter what anyone else will think or how anyone else has done it in the past. It only matters that you do what you want to do—that you act on what has integrity for you.

This may feel very selfish, and in an effort not to be self-centered you may be inclined not to express what you need. But this is a time when energy is depleted and emotions are intense. You have all you can say grace over. This is a time to be selfish.

You certainly can be sensitive and gracious, but focusing on your own needs is imperative. The demands of the moment don't allow you to do otherwise.

Marriage and Family: In It Together

*I bow my knees before the Father, from whom every
family in heaven and on earth takes its name. . . .
being rooted and grounded in love.*
—Ephesians 3:14-15, 17

It was a few days after Patrick had gotten out of his
body cast. I heard a faint sound from the downstairs
bathroom, and then he began crying. I rushed to him. He
had meant simply to place his can of Coke on the edge of
the sink but had missed. It fell into the sink and poured
out.

This seemed the perfect place to spill something. It all
went down the drain. There was no mess. There was liter-
ally nothing to clean up. But Patrick was inconsolable. I
assured him this was not a problem. We had plenty more
Cokes.

Still he sobbed and sobbed. And he was right. There was
a problem. So much had spilled. So much had been lost
that could never be replaced. There was a mess—not in the
sink—in our lives.

I held him close as he cried.

41

I think of a family as a mobile, with the pieces hanging in delicate balance. With the death of a family member, an important piece is suddenly missing. The balance is broken. The stress can be enormous in the wake of the loss. A mobile sways as it seeks to discover a new balance, a new equilibrium. The family is reeling from its grief while it is searching for its new identity.

It is vital that family members be open and supportive of one another as they go through this ordeal. Working together is the only way.

The Marriage

Karen and I went through it together. We talked, we cried, and we cared. Under the stress we could get irritable and on edge, but we tried not to take it out on each other. We each respected the enormous pain the other was feeling. We didn't do it perfectly—we sometimes got on each other's nerves—but we each knew we were married to someone who loved us openly and intentionally.

We slogged through the miles of grief together. Consistently together. Thank God, together.

Grief can be a crucial time for couples. The divorce rate for couples who lose a child is said to be alarmingly high. Under the weight of the pressure of personal loss, any former hairline fracture in the marriage can cause a major split to occur.

My opinion is that a traumatic loss will cause the marriage to be either strengthened or weakened. It depends on many factors, but the biggest is how connected, open, and respectful the couple is with each other. In that regard, let me make some suggestions:

- *Get connected. Stay connected.* If your marriage has never been very personal, this is the time to begin. If your marriage is close, with open communication, this is the time to take that relationship to a deeper level of emotional intimacy.
- *Talk with your spouse about how you are feeling.* Often it is the men who struggle the most with this. As best you can, talk about what this experience is like for you. Open up. Risk being personal. Talk about your memories. Tell your stories. Use this loving relationship to work through your pain. But also respect the times when you need to be quiet, to step back from the effort.
- *Remember to ask often how your partner is doing, and to wait for the answer.* Mean it. *Want* to know. Ask what he or she needs from you right now. Respect what you hear. Sometimes what is needed is an opportunity to pour out the hurt. At other times it is a time of privacy. And sometimes what he or she needs may be simply to take a break—to have dinner, to go to a movie, to be "normal."

If you have never been openly empathic or caring, know that your spouse may need it now as never before.

Listen as your partner opens up with you. Patiently listen. Don't be nervous; no one is expecting—or needing—anything profound from you, only a caring heart and a few minutes of your time, unhurried, with no glancing at your watch. Go through this experience as a couple—knowing you can count on each other.

The Children

Our children need our care and support more than ever following an important loss. They bring their pain, and their honest, direct questions. They often push us to think through issues we had never before considered. Be real with them. Be authentic.

Talk with your children about death with gentleness and patience. Tell them of your faith and belief in God's consistent love and presence. Share with them what eternal life means to you. Feel very free to say "I don't know" when you don't know the answer to a question—since much of death is a mystery to us all. This is honest, and it frees your children to feel all right about themselves as they look into this mystery and feel the same uncertainty. Answer what you know. Yet in all your conversations with them, remember: More than any explanation, they need parents who will be loving, supportive, and with them through it all.

Connect with your children where they are. Do not assume you know how they feel. *Ask* them. What they are experiencing will depend on various factors such as

44

where they are in the developmental process and the nature of their relationship with the one who died. They may not have developed the ability to conceptualize death and its irreversibility, but they will know Grandpa isn't there, and they will need someone to hold them.

Encourage your children to talk with you—when they are ready. Ask them their favorite memories of times with Grandpa. Help them put words on their feelings. You may find they are not as sad as everyone else; or this experience may have affected them in a way you could never have guessed. Invite them to be open with you—whatever they feel—again, when they are ready. Respect that there will be times they want to talk, and times when they do not. The pain may be there now, or it may come later.

Respect any emotion honestly expressed. By not judging, you allow your children freely to pour out from their hearts. Give them permission to be sad or to cry or to be angry or to be quiet or to stay close to you or to be alone—whatever they need. Help them do what you have modeled, to give a voice to their pain.

"How Many Stockings Shall We Hang?"

Even so it is not the will of your Father who is in heaven, that one of these little ones should perish.
—Matthew 18:14 ASV

Patrick was beginning the first grade. Each morning the big yellow bus would rumble down our street and stop to pick him up at the end of our driveway.

It was a sight not to be missed, and the dining-room window offered the best view. So Karen would sit on the floor in front of the very window with all of Eric's markings. Eric would take his place in her lap to watch his big brother. This quickly became their morning tradition.

There they would watch the big event together. Every morning. There they would wave "good-bye" as Patrick took his seat and the bus slowly pulled away.

It was several months after the accident that Patrick's leg was healed. On the first morning he could walk down the driveway, his mom was sitting in her spot at the window, watching, her lap empty. Alone.

47

But every morning she was there. Watching. Waving. Alone.

The pain for this mother was beyond our imagining. And so was her courage.

Many say that the death of a child is the worst. I don't compare losses, since they each are so different. I simply know it is devastating. It has been said the death of a parent is the loss of one's past; the death of a spouse is the loss of one's present; and the death of a child is the loss of one's future.

A child's death feels so unnatural. It is a contradiction to nature. Our children are supposed to bury us, not the other way around. So it tends to be a special loss.

The church in which I grew up has always had a unique tradition when announcing the death of any adult in the congregation. In the church bulletin the announcement would begin with the words, "First United Methodist Church celebrates the completed life of . . ." Those words are so well chosen. There is much satisfaction and celebration in that it was a life lived out to its completion.

A child's death feels so different. A life ending so early, so unexpectedly, feels so unfinished and incomplete. There is much in life that will never be experienced.

Yet, it was a life that was lived—fully, though briefly. It may have been a short life, but it was a beautiful life. As Viktor Frankl wrote in *The Doctor and the Soul*, "We cannot, after all, judge a biography by its length, by the number of pages in it; we must judge by the richness of the contents. . . . Sometimes the 'unfinisheds' are among the most beautiful symphonies" (New York: Vintage, 1986, p. 66).

Every parent who has suffered the loss of a child knows this—which is why it hurts so badly. The brief symphony they had known was rare and beautiful. And so quickly it was over. It is devastating. These parents have many moments when suddenly the pain of that awareness hits them so hard.

It may be a wonderful day in early December. The boxes of Christmas decorations are brought up from the basement and are being unpacked. The moment may happen when you get to the stockings. There it is: your child's name on the top of her Christmas stocking. You turn to your spouse in tears and ask, "What do we do? Do we hang it up with the others? I can't just leave it." Decorating for Christmas suddenly is interrupted by the next wave of a parent's grief.

Or the trigger may be a simple question. For example, in casual conversation, a woman may be asked, "So, how many children do you have?" It's like a knife. The pain is so intense. There is a pause as this mother tries to regroup and get on top of her emotions. *"THREE!"* she wants to shout. *"I HAVE THREE CHILDREN—ONLY, ONE IS DEAD, AND I'LL NEVER HOLD HER AGAIN!"*

"Two," she says. "I have two children. A daughter and a son." And the conversation goes politely along as if this dear woman isn't emotionally doubled over in pain. She could have graciously answered either way—politely or more truthfully—with integrity. This questioner was a stranger whom she likely would never see again, so she gave the social response. The world is not a therapy group, so this was a valid choice.

Yet deep within her is the sense that she has just lied. *Three.* She will always have *three* children.

Karen handled it so well in a different context. She was meeting for the first time with a group of teachers with whom she would be working. Many of them did not know one another, so they were going around the room introducing themselves. When it was her turn she said, "My name is Karen Greer. I'm married to Ron. We have three children, two of whom we have been privileged to be able to keep."

As if They Never Lived

These things I remember, / as I pour out my soul.
—Psalm 42:4

As I write this it has been over two decades since Eric died. Through all those years, nearly every Christmas something remarkable happens. When we get our bundle of gifts shipped by my brother and sister-in-law, there is one extra gift in the package. It is often an angel or a candle.*

There may be no name on it, or it may say simply, "For Eric." We are always touched by the warmth of feeling so loved. We hang the angel ornament or light the candle with gratitude that someone out there remembered Eric lived.

It is painful enough to have someone die whom you so loved. It is almost as painful to have them treated as if they had never lived. Nearly anyone who has been through an intimate, personal grief knows this dynamic too well. A child of five dies or a marriage of fifty-five years suddenly ends in death. After a relatively brief period—often days or weeks—in which memories are shared, the name is then almost never spoken. From the tone of subsequent conversations it is as if this very important person had never lived.

The next extended-family gathering can come and go and the name is not once uttered. "I didn't want to upset Ethel. She's still struggling with his dying, you know." Well, that seems to me to be reason *for* sharing stories and memories, and inviting Ethel to do the same. Healing seems to come more readily from opening up in trusted, loving relationships.

Just to hear the name spoken of one's dead child or late husband has the opposite effect of the reaction feared. It is hardly going to "remind" them of their pain. Especially early on, they are thinking of little else. It is going to say to them that they are not alone—someone else is also thinking of this person they so loved. He did exist, and you are remembering him, too. Just to hear the name spoken is an absolute joy. Someone has entered your world. You are no longer alone.

Last Words

"How forceful are honest words!" —Job 6:25a

Our children's favorite sitter, Debbie, had just been picked up. She had a new hairstyle and was receiving compliments from all in the car. Eric strained to look around to see her from his car seat in the front. When he did, he smiled and said, "Pretty, Debbie."

Those were his final words.

The final moments of a relationship can take on an incredible significance. They may be replayed again and again. They may be examined repeatedly to glean all the meaning that can be found.

I talk with so many people following the death of someone profoundly important to them and hear them agonize over how the relationship ended. Often the regret is deep because their last words were not "I love you." Rarely are the words that were spoken hostile or mean-spirited; they simply were not words of love. It is understandable that anyone would want to say good-bye with the most caring words being spoken.

Yet, my last words to Eric were hardly kind and gentle. I last spoke to him late in the evening from the bottom of the stairs to the top with the words, "If you don't get back in that bed this very minute, I'm going to come up there and put you in it!"

Those were my last words. But unlike others might, I feel neither remorse nor shame. In fact, those final words feel solid to me. I was loving my son to the very end of his life. In the context of a two-year-old boy having gotten out of bed for the third time, anything else would have been poor parenting. My words were not words of love, but they were loving words.

There is a higher priority than parting with some magical phrase, and that is to be in the middle of a loving relationship right to the end. Naturally, there may be regrets with which we have to live. But if that relationship happens to be in the middle of an argument, still working for resolution, then that loved one knew he or she mattered enough for you to keep working at it.

Life simply isn't neat. It is lived out in real situations that often are not of our choosing. Sometimes it gets messy. Relationships become strained. Anger may be expressed. Feelings can get hurt. And right in the middle of the whole mess, someone dies. Life isn't neat. But that doesn't mean we were less than loving when suddenly we had to say good-bye.

Yet, in my office someone may describe a different life story. A man may tell me that when his sister died the relationship was in a very ugly place. Hostile words, meant to hurt, had been spoken, followed by years of speaking not a single word. Then came the phone call: Sis had died unexpectedly during the night, and the arrangements were being made.

He had always thought that one day these two "stubborn old fools" would talk it out and get the relationship back on track—but not now. The anticipated reunion will never happen. The guilt and remorse he feels are, at times, overwhelming.

So what should he do? How should he work through this maze of emotion in which he feels so lost and so stuck? Likely, he should get professional help. He needs to talk this out with someone who knows the issues and can help him work through them. There are no quick and easy answers. This has to be talked through.

The guilt of his participation can't be glossed over or he will live with the burden of it for the rest of his life. It has to be addressed. If he and his sister were each acting like a couple of children, he also will want to look into that part of himself that had him relating with such immaturity.

Ultimately, he will need to get to the place that he can forgive himself and can forgive her. He then can say "good-bye" and move ahead, having grown and been transformed by the experience.

If your relationship ended with severe regret, in whatever fashion, do not bury it or distract yourself from it. Courageously, look it squarely in the eye. Address it now. Get whatever help you need. Do not allow yourself to become paralyzed, to get stuck here. Free yourself from it. There is too much life to be lived.

Supporting Those Who Grieve

Like vinegar on a wound
is one who sings songs to a heavy heart.
—Proverbs 25:20

*ell-meaning and loving people want to speak a kind
word that will make a difference. "Well, isn't it good to
know that Eric is in his heavenly Father's care right now?"
Yes and no. Of course, it's a tremendous relief. But, no, it
doesn't feel so hot at just this moment. He was still to be in
this father's care.*

*I was looking for connection. Not to feel better. Nothing
could do that. Rather, I needed to be cared for in my hurt.
"Ron, I know this is a living nightmare for you. It couldn't
be worse. I am so sorry." That's all. That's all I needed.
That's all anyone really needs. Not pretty words. Just honest understanding.*

I regularly talk with those who want to help friends
who are struggling, but who genuinely don't know what
would be helpful. This is so important, for it is well doc-
umented that persons who are supported by family and

friends are the ones who most successfully work through their grief. In both this reflection and in the one that follows, I want to write to those who want to be supportive but who are uncertain of the most effective and loving ways. Here are some directions.

Have the courage to stay close and the wisdom to be honest. The pain of those who hurt can be so great, that some can't stand to stay near it. Many of these are good, well-meaning people. But in their anxiety and in not knowing what to say or do, they back away. They may send a card, and even flowers, but there are no calls or personal visits.

People often say, "I miss my child, but I also miss my friends."

Stay in the game. Stay in the relationship. They need you now like never before. Love them, and let them know it. When you visit, connect emotionally.

Some may make the visit but not realize the emotional distance they are keeping. Instead of truly connecting with those who are grieving, they may pull out "hopeful words." On one level they are wanting to be helpful. On another they are trying to talk those in pain out of their grief instead of joining them in it.

Proverbs 25:20 says it bluntly and clearly: "Like vinegar on a wound / is one who sings songs to a heavy heart."

Someone said to me the day after Eric died, "Well, at least you had two wonderful years with him." Though true, it was not well timed. That was not my focus at the moment. I responded, "You're right. But all I can think of now is the years I won't have with him."

Words of hope are tricky. Properly timed, they boost the spirit and brighten one's perspective. Poorly timed, they leave one feeling very alone. Good news isn't good news when it comes too soon in this process. Early on in one's pain, what is needed is support, closeness, understanding—not cheerleading.

To those who "don't know what to say," please know it doesn't really matter what one says as long as it is under the broad umbrella of "I love you, and I'm so sorry you are having to go through this."

Any affirmation to those grieving must be genuine. If not, they will feel it. No matter how well intended, they need nothing phony, nothing overstated. It will erode trust. Or in the unusual case when they do believe a Pollyanna story, their hope will be inflated just as reality forces them to crash and burn—leaving them in even worse shape. But usually, they will feel alone.

Sometimes it gives more hope to the one who is struggling to have it confirmed just how bad it is. It helps to know that one isn't as crazy as one feels—that it really does hurt that badly.

What matters is that you care enough to be with them—that you came to see them when there are no words to speak that will make them feel better. It's not your words, it's your presence that matters. If you have compassion, it will show. The word *compassion* finds its origin in the Latin word *pati*, which means both "to suffer" and "to endure." It points to caring for the long haul. It means to suffer with another, to join in the struggle with patience and without hurry.

As we respond with compassion, we respond with empathy and with patience. It is the rare—and valued— friend who will remember the following year to send a card on the anniversary of her husband's death. She will be touched beyond words. Only when one has been the recipient of intentional caring does he or she know the power of that intimacy. It is the gift of being received with an acceptance of who you are, where you are.

What one needs in the depth of the pain is honest support. As Paul put it, we must speak "the truth in love" (Ephesians 4:15). The truth is needed—yet spoken lovingly. "It's going to be a tough road. But I know you, and I know you will make it. You will have a wonderful life again one day. I just wish it were going to be sooner than you and I know it will be." This tells them the difficult truth, but it also tells them you believe in them and are with them. Now, that brings genuine hope.

What greater gift can be given than the nearness of a loving friend who accepts you where you are—without trying to change you or hurry you out of your pain. "I am so sorry this happened to you" or "Please know how terribly saddened we are for you" is all that is needed. Simply express how you feel. "I love you," is quite enough. And it is such a gift.

Care Enough to Listen

Let everyone be quick to listen, slow to speak.
—James 1:19

I n the hour following the accident our sons were taken from the emergency room of one hospital to be admitted into another. A friend drove me. It took twenty minutes or so. He let me sit in silence, processing, digesting the bits of information I had just been told about the accident and everyone's condition. I made a comment or two to which he kindly listened. He let me sit in the silence and said not a word.

Not a single word.

The single greatest gift a grieving person can receive is to be heard, to be given the opportunity to talk and talk and talk out the pain. Another gift is for someone simply to be there in the silence when there is nothing left to say.

This pain can't be fixed. It can only be worked through—and they need your company and support like never before as they engage that task. They need to hear

"How are you doing?" from someone who really wants to know and who is going to patiently listen. Get them to tell their stories. Invite them to remember with you about the memories and the times they shared with this special person.

Silence is rarely given its due. In this context it means we temporarily set aside our needs in order to be with them in theirs. It means we care enough to listen, both in order to learn and to give them the opportunity to tell their story. Our willingness to listen also quietly tells them that they are valued, their story is worth hearing, and we are genuinely interested.

As the writer of Ecclesiastes put it, there is "a time to keep silence, and a time to speak" (3:7b). Our presence in their grief will speak more compassionately than any words.

I have heard many times from those who have been through a personal heartache of how important the support has been of those who cared. "I couldn't have made it without them," is how it is often expressed.

Rarely do they quote anything that was said. If something profound was spoken, that was not what touched them. It's not *what* they heard; it was that they *were* heard. It had more to do with the other's presence and willingness to listen.

Patrick needed to talk with Karen for the first several nights following the accident. Each evening he would recount a part of the experience they had been through. He needed to talk with his mama and no one else. He needed her only to listen. He needed to try to get his arms around what had happened, to put it in its place in his memory. The last of these nights he spoke of the kind man beside the highway who was so gentle and caring. He did not talk of the accident again for months.

We each can remember when we were at similar points in our lives. Remember what you needed and didn't need when you were there? You probably needed, above all else, to know that you were not alone—you needed someone patiently to listen to you. What you likely did not need was for someone to get in your way. What you did not need was for someone to interrupt your working through what you had to work through.

So why is it that most need to talk so much, to "get it out" after a heartbreak? The event that has brought such pain has infused them with emotional input. This leaves them in a state of imbalance. To regain equilibrium they must balance the input with output. Thus, they need to give it a voice. They need to find ways to express their pain and grief and rage at the tragedy that has torn apart their lives.

These painful emotions emerge only after there is enough room for them, uncluttered by words and agendas imposed on them. Thus the need for quiet, intentional listening. Unlike social conversation where we are often thinking what we are going to say next, here what is more relevant is what we are going to *ask* next.

Professional counseling can be helpful but is not needed for most heartaches. What is needed is someone caring enough to visit, courageous enough to ask how the heart-broken person is feeling, and wise enough to be quiet and listen.

A Strength and a Spirit

*You shall no longer be called Jacob, but Israel,
for you have striven with God and with humans,
and have prevailed. —Genesis 32:28*

Karen said to me a few weeks after Eric's death, *"We're going to make it through this and have fun and enjoy ourselves again. Because if we don't, then Eric will not have been the only one who died."*

And we came back—no, we moved on to a new place. We moved through it to a place we had never been before. We had to go down and draw on resources heretofore untouched. We discovered more about God and ourselves than we had ever known.

As I write this, Eric would have been twenty-one years old this past August. It's hard to believe that so many years have passed since his death. On each of his birthdays I go to the cemetery instead of going to a party.

On those special days it still hurts—badly. And it always will. Make no mistake, I have grieved as thoroughly, as often, and as well as I know how to do it. It is not because of repressed grief that the wound is yet fully to close—but because of the magnitude of the loss.

The Scriptures tell us that Jacob came out of his long, dark night of the soul by the River Jabbok with a limp (Genesis 32:22-32). He had been wrestling throughout those dark hours, and his hip had been thrown out of joint. We know about those nights. Isn't it true for all of us that in the darkness we struggle with life's deepest matters? We don't know the exact nature of that struggle for Jacob. From his story we have ideas, but the intimate details will forever remain between him and God.

Yet, we know all that we need to know from his story. In fact, we know more than we wish we knew. We have lived the story. His long, dark night is ours. His wound is our wound. He limps a lot like we do.

Jacob would be aware of this wound for the rest of his life. My wound may be different from his, but I always resonate with that passage and with that limp.

The Scriptures didn't say he would always be in pain with it, only perhaps on certain days, when the weather does a number on aching joints. Nor did they say it slowed him down. Mostly it was an awareness of where he had been and what he had been through—which hurt every so often.

That's the way it seems to be with deep losses and old wounds. A widow of thirty years tears up as she speaks of the day she and her husband met and began falling in love. A man pauses in mid-sentence to catch his breath as he talks of his mother, whom he lost as a child.

Did they not grieve enough? Was too much tucked away and repressed? Perhaps. Or maybe the loss was so profound, the wound so deep that they will always walk with a hint of a limp. Those tender moments are such an affirmation of what was and always will be.

Yet, Jacob met the sunrise with more than a bum hip. He also had a new name. He had a new identity. In some important ways, Jacob—*Israel*, that is—was a new person. For those who don't run from their dark nights by the river, for those who instead engage the struggle before them, there is a change that takes place. It may be either subtle or apparent, but it is true of any who are forced by life's circumstances to go within themselves, to where they had never been before.

They face the morning light with a depth, a grounding, an awareness of so much more that God had placed within them. The words of Ernest Hemingway from *A Farewell to Arms* come to mind: "The world breaks every one and afterward many are strong at the broken places" (New York: Scribner, 1929, p. 249).

At times I feel guilty as to how much I have grown from this experience. Out of tragedy we learn of what we are made. We each have had to call on spiritual and emotional resources we had never known before. There is a confidence that comes from knowing that tragedy may knock us down, but it will not overwhelm us. We go through the rest of our lives grounded by the depth and substance that is within us. It is ironic that God is found more personally in the darkness of the night than in the brightness of the day.

Dr. Harry Emerson Fosdick wrote, "In my young manhood I had a critical nervous breakdown. It is the most terrifying wilderness I've ever traveled through. I dreadfully wanted to commit suicide but instead I made some of the most vital discoveries of my life. . . . I found God in the desert. Why is it that some of life's most revealing insights come to us not from life's loveliness but from life's difficulties?" (*What Is Vital Religion?* [New York: Harper and Brothers, 1955], p. 9).

Sometimes when working with persons who have experienced profound loss—as they are feeling stronger and the pain less acute—I will ask them, "In a strange way, do you ever feel as if it's the rest of the world that has been cheated?" Not once have they failed to smile a smile of recognition, knowing exactly what I meant. They bring more depth and more maturity to their lives. They are more substantial persons because of having been where they were forced to go.

This is certainly the truth to which Paul was pointing in Romans when he wrote, "Suffering produces endurance, and endurance produces character, and character produces hope, and hope does not disappoint us" (5:3-5).

I may climb the hill at the cemetery with a limp on that afternoon each August. But I climb it, also, with a strength and a spirit I brought with me out of the long, dark night.

Sacred Moments

For truly to see your face is like seeing the face of God. —Genesis 33:10

I remember so well playing with our two sons on that particular evening, years ago. They liked to lie down on the floor, put their feet in the air, and have me pick them up by the ankles and swing them around. After a while Patrick tired of it and went back to the television. Eric never seemed to tire of it. "More, Daddy, more," he would say. And so Daddy picked him up and swung him until his arms insisted on "no more."

It was a fun evening. Karen got home from choir practice, we popped some popcorn, and we enjoyed the time together. It was a good evening. It was a relaxed evening. Of course, we were not to know that it was to be our last evening together.

That last evening has become for me a sacred evening. Those moments together—our last moments—are sacred moments.

Yet, one wonders, if Eric had not died, would those moments have been any less sacred? Of course not. The only difference is that I would not have looked upon them as being as rich and deep and valuable as in fact they were. I would have missed seeing the beauty of that wonderful time together.

Life is filled with just such moments. In the midst of the boring and the mundane, there are, scattered throughout our lives, sacred moments—moments when God's grace is felt and known.

These are moments when we can identify with Jacob as he spoke to his brother Esau, "For truly to see your face is like seeing the face of God." We all have been there.

We have looked into the loving eyes of our children as they felt, and sometimes voiced, their appreciation for our being there for them. We have felt the grace when our spouses overlooked the wrong they had every right to have held against us. Or perhaps it was just a delightful family evening enjoying those who matter the most, popping popcorn and kicking back. We have had countless moments when in the faces of those we love it was "like seeing the face of God."

Perhaps the losses we experience in life help us recognize these precious times with those we love—to value them and make the most of them. As Alfred Lord Tennyson wrote, "Though much is taken, much abides."

At our home we have moved forward with a new clarity of what truly matters in life and what does not. We see through that glass less darkly, with an awareness of how sacred life, and each of its precious moments, really is. We tend to hug those we love a little tighter and a lot more often.

Epilogue

I was again at the window. It was four years after Eric died. Much had happened over that time. Our daughter, Brooke, was born. Patrick was now in the fourth grade. After much deliberation, Karen and I decided it was time for us to move, to be nearer Patrick's school and my office.

The move had taken place that day. I had gone back in the evening to pick up the inevitable things we had left and had taken them to the car. I walked back into the house one final time.

Much like the earlier visit to our home, Eric was very much on my mind. It had not been his home for long, but it was the last home we would share with him. All of his things that we had kept had been moved—except his window.

There it was again. Eric's markings were etched into the woodwork. I sat on the floor, and my fingers followed those lines one last time. For the life of me, I wanted to get a crowbar, rip it off the wall and take it with me.

Instead, through my tears, I left with the grace of the countless memories and joys Eric had marked on the window into my soul.

CPSIA information can be obtained at www.ICGtesting.com
Printed in the USA
LVOW101142181212

312222LV00006B/155/P